The CrowdStrike Outage of 2024

Understanding the Breakdown and Building Better Practices, Strategies for Prevention, Recovery, and Enhanced Cybersecurity

Vertex Publishing

Copyright

Table of Contents

Chapter 1: Introduction to the Incident

Overview of CrowdStrike Outage

On July 19, 2024, a significant outage impacted numerous systems globally due to a defect in a recent content update from CrowdStrike. This update, specifically targeting Windows hosts, resulted in widespread system crashes and blue screen errors, causing considerable disruption to various sectors, including state governments, healthcare, and transportation.

The defect was isolated to a single update for the Falcon Sensor product, affecting only Windows systems, with Mac and Linux hosts remaining unaffected. CrowdStrike quickly identified and addressed the issue, deploying a fix to restore normal operations. Despite the rapid response, the outage had already caused significant downtime and operational challenges.

CrowdStrike, a leading cybersecurity firm known for its Falcon platform, which provides next-generation endpoint protection, took immediate action by working closely with impacted customers and partners to ensure all systems were restored. The company assured users that this incident was not a cyberattack but a result of an internal software defect. As part of their response, CrowdStrike has committed to providing continuous updates through their support portal and blog, emphasizing their dedication to transparency and customer support during this recovery process.

The outage has highlighted the critical dependence on cybersecurity and IT infrastructure in maintaining operational continuity across various sectors. It also underscored the importance of robust update testing and quick response mechanisms to mitigate the impact of such incidents.

Initial Acknowledgment by CrowdStrike

On July 19, 2024, CrowdStrike experienced a significant outage due to a defect found in a content update for its Falcon sensor on Windows hosts. The issue was not related to a cyberattack but stemmed from a problematic software update. Mac and Linux hosts were unaffected. The company moved swiftly to identify and isolate the issue, deploying a fix and ensuring impacted systems were being restored.

CrowdStrike's CEO, George Kurtz, addressed the situation with a public statement. He expressed sincere apologies for the inconvenience caused by the outage and reassured customers that the company was prioritizing system restoration. Kurtz emphasized that CrowdStrike's Falcon platform and its services, such as Falcon Complete and Falcon OverWatch, were operating normally and that the protection provided by the Falcon sensor was not compromised.

To maintain transparency and provide ongoing support, CrowdStrike directed affected customers to their Support Portal and official blog for continuous updates. Kurtz encouraged customers to remain vigilant against potential exploitation by adversaries during the incident, urging them to engage only with official CrowdStrike representatives.

The company mobilized its resources to assist affected customers, offering technical support and guidance through established communication channels. CrowdStrike's commitment to resolving the incident included providing detailed information on the issue, its impact, and the steps being taken to prevent similar occurrences in the future.

Chapter 2: Technical Details of the Outage

Identification and Isolation of the Defect

The technical issue that led to the CrowdStrike outage was identified as a defect within a content update for the Falcon sensor, specifically affecting Windows hosts. This section will delve into how CrowdStrike's engineering and technical teams worked to pinpoint and address the defect.

1. Detection of the Issue:

On July 19, 2024, reports began surfacing of widespread system crashes and blue screen errors on Windows hosts utilizing the Falcon sensor. These reports were quickly escalated to CrowdStrike's technical support and engineering teams, who initiated an investigation to determine the root cause of the issue.

2. Initial Investigation:

The investigation revealed that the problem was linked to a specific content update file within the Falcon sensor update. The problematic file was identified as "C-00000291*.sys" with a timestamp of 0409 UTC. Systems that received this file began exhibiting severe stability issues, including bugcheck errors and repeated blue screens.

3. Isolation of the Defect:

CrowdStrike's engineers isolated the defective update to prevent further propagation. They reverted the content update to a previous stable version, with the corrected file timestamped at 0527 UTC. This quick action helped to mitigate additional impacts on systems that had not yet applied the faulty update.

4. Deployment of the Fix:

With the defect isolated, CrowdStrike immediately worked on deploying a fix. The fix involved pushing out a new update that included the stable version of the "C-00000291*.sys" file. Additionally, CrowdStrike provided detailed instructions and workaround steps for systems that were unable to receive the automatic update due to continuous crashes.

5. Communication and Coordination:

CrowdStrike maintained open lines of communication with its customers, providing real-time updates through their Support Portal and official blog. They advised customers on how to verify the presence of the problematic file and the correct procedure to delete it if necessary. CrowdStrike also coordinated with various stakeholders, including federal and state agencies, to ensure a comprehensive response to the incident.

6. Monitoring and Assurance:

Following the deployment of the fix, CrowdStrike's teams closely monitored the situation to ensure that the issue was fully resolved. They assured customers that the Falcon platform itself remained secure and that the protection offered by the Falcon sensor was not compromised. Continuous updates and support were provided to help customers restore normal operations swiftly.

In summary, the identification and isolation of the defect within the Falcon content update involved a systematic investigation, swift corrective actions, and thorough communication with affected parties. This proactive approach underscored CrowdStrike's commitment to maintaining system stability and customer trust during the outage.

Affected Systems and Platforms

The CrowdStrike outage, which began on July 19, 2024, primarily impacted Windows-based systems. This issue arose from a defect in a content update for the Falcon sensor, a critical component of CrowdStrike's endpoint protection solution. The defect caused widespread disruptions in Windows environments but did not affect Mac or Linux hosts.

Affected Systems:

- **Windows Hosts:** The primary impact was observed on Windows 10 and later versions. The faulty update led to blue screen errors and system crashes on some Windows hosts. These issues were specifically linked to a problematic content update file associated with the Falcon sensor.

- **State Government Systems:** In Maryland, the outage affected various state government operations, causing minimal disruption across most agencies. However, some departments, including Health and Transportation, experienced significant technical issues due to the faulty update.

- **Public and Private Sector Systems:** The incident also affected critical infrastructure and business operations. Airlines operating out of Baltimore/Washington International Thurgood Marshall Airport faced disruptions, and toll transaction processing with Maryland EZPass experienced delays.

Non-Affected Platforms:

- **Mac and Linux Hosts:** CrowdStrike confirmed that the update issue did not impact systems running macOS or Linux. These platforms continued to operate normally without experiencing the same disruptions as Windows systems.

Resolution Efforts:

CrowdStrike rapidly identified and isolated the defect, deploying a fix to address the issue. They also provided detailed guidance and workarounds for affected Windows hosts to restore normal operations. The company's technical support teams worked closely with impacted customers to ensure a swift resolution.

Detailed Symptomatology and Error Reports

The technical issues caused by the CrowdStrike Falcon sensor update were marked by specific symptoms and errors on affected systems. Here is a detailed breakdown:

1. Symptoms Experienced by Affected Systems

- **Bugcheck/Blue Screen Errors:** Many Windows hosts exhibited blue screen errors (also known as "bugcheck" errors) directly linked to the Falcon sensor. These errors resulted in system crashes and interruptions in normal operations.

- **System Crashes:** The Falcon sensor update led to frequent and unexpected system crashes. These crashes rendered affected systems unstable and unusable, prompting the need for immediate remediation.

- **Service Disruption:** Organizations reported disruptions in their IT services due to these crashes. In some cases, critical business processes and operations were impacted, causing delays and operational inefficiencies.

2. Error Reports and Technical Details

- **Channel File Timestamps:** The issue was traced to a specific channel file, "C-00000291*.sys." The problematic version of this file had a timestamp of 0409 UTC, while the reverted, non-problematic version had a timestamp of 0527 UTC. Affected systems contained the faulty file version, leading to the observed errors.

- **File Identification:** Users could identify the problematic file by navigating to the CrowdStrike directory under `%WINDIR%\System32\drivers\CrowdStrike`. The presence of files with timestamps prior to 0527 UTC indicated the outdated and faulty update.

- **Error Patterns:** Detailed error reports revealed that the issue was not uniform; some systems experienced immediate crashes upon the update, while others had intermittent stability problems.

The patterns of these errors provided insights into the timing and extent of the impact.

3. Impact on System Operations

- **Recovery Challenges:** Systems that had been impacted were challenging to recover, particularly if they were unable to download the reverted channel file automatically. Manual intervention was often required to address the issues and restore normal operation.

- **Temporary Workarounds:** Several workarounds were suggested for systems still experiencing issues, including rebooting systems into Safe Mode, manually deleting the faulty file, and ensuring systems were on a wired network for faster recovery.

4. Ongoing Monitoring and Support

- **Technical Alerts:** CrowdStrike provided continuous technical alerts and updates through their Support Portal and blog. These updates included detailed instructions for identifying and mitigating the issues caused by the faulty update.

- **Customer Support:** Dedicated support teams were available to assist affected organizations, offering guidance on resolving the issues and implementing the necessary fixes.

By addressing these symptoms and providing detailed error reports, CrowdStrike aimed to help organizations navigate the impacts of the outage and ensure a swift and effective recovery.

Chapter 3: Immediate Response and Fix Deployment

CrowdStrike's Actions and Fix Deployment

In response to the widespread issues caused by the faulty Falcon sensor update, CrowdStrike took several critical actions to address the problem and deploy a fix. Here's a detailed overview of their immediate response and the steps taken to resolve the outage:

1. Detection and Identification

- **Issue Identification:** CrowdStrike swiftly identified the root cause of the outage—a defect in the Falcon sensor content update. This identification was crucial in isolating the problem and determining the appropriate corrective measures.

- **Impact Assessment:** The company assessed the extent of the impact, confirming that the issue affected Windows hosts but did not impact Mac or Linux systems. This assessment helped focus the response efforts on the affected platforms.

2. Fix Deployment

- **Reversion of Problematic Update:** Once the defect was identified, CrowdStrike reverted the faulty content update. The problematic channel file, identified by its timestamp of 0409 UTC, was replaced with a reverted version that had a timestamp of 0527 UTC. This reversion aimed to restore normal functionality to affected systems.

- **Automatic Update Rollout:** CrowdStrike initiated an automatic update to deploy the fixed channel file across all affected Windows hosts. This update was designed to address the issue without requiring manual intervention in most cases.

- **Manual Intervention:** For systems unable to receive the automatic update, CrowdStrike provided detailed instructions for manual intervention. This included steps to navigate to the relevant directory, delete the faulty file, and reboot the system to apply the fix.

3. Communication and Support

- **Customer Communication:** CrowdStrike maintained open lines of communication with affected customers through their Support Portal and blog. They provided real-time updates on the status of the fix deployment and additional guidance on addressing any remaining issues.

- **Technical Support:** A dedicated support team was mobilized to assist organizations in resolving the issues. This included providing one-on-one support to affected customers and guiding them through the troubleshooting and recovery process.

4. Monitoring and Follow-Up

- **Continuous Monitoring:** CrowdStrike implemented continuous monitoring to ensure the fix was successfully applied and to detect any residual issues. This proactive approach helped in quickly addressing any further problems that arose during the recovery phase.

- **Post-Incident Review:** After the immediate response, CrowdStrike conducted a thorough review of the incident. This review aimed to understand the root cause of the defect, assess the effectiveness of the response, and implement measures to prevent similar issues in the future.

Through these coordinated actions, CrowdStrike aimed to minimize the disruption caused by the outage and ensure a swift restoration of services for affected organizations. The company's response demonstrated a commitment to resolving the issue promptly and maintaining transparency throughout the process.

Recommendations for Impacted Customers

For organizations affected by the CrowdStrike Falcon sensor update outage, following structured recommendations can help mitigate disruptions and ensure a smooth recovery. Here are key recommendations for impacted customers:

1. Immediate Actions for Affected Systems

- **Verify the Update Status:** Check if the system is running the problematic version of the Falcon sensor update by inspecting the channel file timestamp in the `%WINDIR%\System32\drivers\CrowdStrike` directory. Ensure that files have the reverted timestamp of 0527 UTC or later.

- **Apply Workarounds:** If the system is still experiencing crashes, follow these workarounds:

- **Reboot into Safe Mode:** Restart the system in Safe Mode or Windows Recovery Environment to stabilize the system.

- **Delete Faulty Files:** Navigate to the CrowdStrike directory and delete any channel files with timestamps before 0527 UTC. Ensure no other files are altered.

- **Cold Boot the Host:** Perform a full shutdown of the host and restart it to allow the system to download the corrected update automatically.

2. System Restoration and Monitoring

- **Monitor System Performance:** After applying fixes, closely monitor system performance and stability to ensure that the issue has been fully resolved.

- **Check for Automatic Updates:** Confirm that the system has received and applied the automatic fix from CrowdStrike. Regularly check for any further updates or patches provided by the vendor.

3. Communication and Coordination

- **Engage with CrowdStrike Support:** Utilize the CrowdStrike Support Portal for the latest updates and detailed instructions. Engage with your CrowdStrike representative or technical support for personalized assistance.

- **Notify Stakeholders:** Inform internal teams and external stakeholders about the situation and any potential impacts. Ensure that communication lines are clear and that stakeholders are aware of the steps being taken to resolve the issue.

4. Review and Enhance Security Measures

- **Strengthen Security Protocols:** Given the possibility of adversaries exploiting the situation, review and enhance cybersecurity measures. Ensure that robust defenses are in place to protect against phishing and other malicious activities.

- **Educate and Train Staff:** Remind employees to be vigilant against phishing attempts and suspicious activities. Conduct training sessions to reinforce cybersecurity best practices and response procedures.

5. Future Preparedness

- **Backup and Recovery Plans:** Review and update backup and recovery plans to ensure quick recovery from similar incidents in the future. Regularly test these plans to maintain preparedness.

- **System Updates and Testing:** Implement a testing phase for future updates to identify potential issues before they affect operational systems. Utilize staging environments to verify the impact of updates in a controlled setting.

6. Stay Informed and Updated

- **Monitor Official Channels:** Continuously check CrowdStrike's blog and Support Portal for ongoing updates and detailed information about the incident and resolution steps.

- **Follow CISA Alerts:** Stay updated with alerts and guidance from CISA and other relevant cybersecurity authorities to ensure comprehensive protection and response.

By adhering to these recommendations, organizations can effectively manage the impacts of the outage, restore normal operations, and enhance their overall cybersecurity posture.

Chapter 4. Official Statements and Public Communication

CrowdStrike's Official Statement and Apology

On July 19, 2024, CrowdStrike issued an official statement addressing the widespread IT outage caused by a defect in a recent Falcon content update for Windows hosts. The company, led by CEO George Kurtz, expressed deep regret over the incident and its impact on customers. Here's a detailed breakdown of CrowdStrike's official statement and apology:

1. Acknowledgment of the Issue

- **Recognition of the Problem:** CrowdStrike acknowledged the severity of the outage affecting Windows hosts due to a faulty content update. The statement clarified that Mac and Linux hosts were not impacted, and assured that the issue was not the result of a cyberattack.

- **Apology to Customers:** CEO George Kurtz extended a sincere apology to customers and partners for the disruption caused. The company recognized the gravity of the situation and the inconvenience experienced by affected organizations.

2. Identification and Resolution

- **Issue Identification:** The statement detailed that the defect in the content update was quickly identified and isolated. CrowdStrike's technical team worked diligently to deploy a fix and resolve the issue.

- **Deployment of Fix:** CrowdStrike assured that the problematic update had been reverted and that a corrected version was being pushed out to affected systems. The company committed to continuous efforts in restoring normal operations and minimizing further disruptions.

3. Assurance of Ongoing Support

- **Commitment to Customer Support:** The statement emphasized CrowdStrike's commitment to supporting affected customers throughout the resolution process. The company highlighted its mobilized team working to assist organizations in recovering and restoring their systems.

- **Availability of Resources:** Customers were directed to the CrowdStrike Support Portal and blog for ongoing updates and guidance. The company encouraged customers to reach out to their CrowdStrike representatives or Technical Support for additional assistance.

4. Focus on Transparency and Future Prevention

- **Commitment to Transparency:** CrowdStrike pledged to provide full transparency regarding the incident, including an explanation of how the issue occurred and steps taken to prevent similar occurrences in the future.

- **Future Prevention Measures:** The statement included a promise to implement measures to prevent such issues from happening again. CrowdStrike outlined plans for reviewing and enhancing their update processes and quality control measures.

5. Vigilance Against Exploitation

- **Encouragement for Vigilance:** Recognizing that adversaries might exploit the situation, CrowdStrike advised customers to remain vigilant against phishing attempts and other malicious activities. The company stressed the importance of engaging with official CrowdStrike representatives and following guidance from trusted sources.

CrowdStrike's statement and apology were designed to address the immediate concerns of affected customers, provide reassurance of the company's commitment to resolving the issue, and outline steps to prevent future incidents. The communication aimed to restore confidence in CrowdStrike's services and support.

Communication Channels and Support Information

In the wake of the CrowdStrike Falcon sensor update outage, effective communication channels and support resources are crucial for managing the incident and addressing customer concerns. Here's a detailed overview of the available communication and support options:

1. CrowdStrike Support Portal

- **Access:** The CrowdStrike Support Portal is the primary channel for accessing real-time updates, technical support, and detailed guidance related to the outage. Customers can log in at [CrowdStrike Support Portal](https://supportportal.crowdstrike.com/s/login/).

- **Features:** The portal provides access to the latest technical alerts, workaround instructions, and system restoration guidance. It also offers a knowledge base with troubleshooting articles and FAQs.

- **Support Requests:** Users can submit support tickets, request assistance, and track the status of their inquiries through the portal.

2. CrowdStrike Blog

- **Access:** Regular updates and official statements from CrowdStrike are posted on their blog. Visit [CrowdStrike Blog](https://www.crowdstrike.com/blog/stateme

nt-on-windows-sensor-update/) for ongoing information and updates.

- **Content:** The blog features detailed articles about the incident, including technical details, recovery steps, and company statements. It serves as a comprehensive source for understanding the nature of the issue and the company's response.

3. Customer Representatives

- **Direct Contact:** Organizations are encouraged to reach out directly to their designated CrowdStrike representatives for personalized support and guidance. Representatives can provide specific assistance based on the customer's setup and requirements.

- **Communication:** Customers should ensure they are communicating through official CrowdStrike channels to avoid misinformation and potential phishing attempts.

4. Technical Support

- **Contact Details:** For immediate technical assistance, customers can contact CrowdStrike Technical Support. The contact information is

available on the CrowdStrike Support Portal and includes phone support, email support, and chat options.
- **Support Hours:** Technical support is available 24/7 to address urgent issues and provide timely resolutions.

5. Public Alerts and Advisories

- **CISA Alerts:** The Cybersecurity and Infrastructure Security Agency (CISA) has issued public alerts regarding the outage. Organizations should monitor CISA's [website](https://www.cisa.gov/) for additional guidance and updates related to the incident.

- **Other Security Agencies:** Updates from international cybersecurity agencies, such as the National Cyber Security Centre (NCSC-UK) and the Australian Cyber Security Centre (ACSC), may also be relevant. Check their respective websites for further information.

6. Social Media

- **CrowdStrike Social Media:** Follow CrowdStrike on social media platforms like Twitter, LinkedIn, and Facebook for timely updates and announcements. CrowdStrike uses these channels to disseminate information quickly and engage with the community.

- **CISA Social Media:** CISA also provides updates via social media, which can be a valuable resource for real-time information and recommendations.

7. Email Notifications

- **Subscriptions:** Ensure that your organization is subscribed to CrowdStrike's email notifications to receive important updates and alerts directly in your inbox.

- **Alerts and Updates:** These emails provide information on critical updates, incident resolutions, and additional resources.

By utilizing these communication channels and support resources, organizations can stay informed, access necessary support, and navigate the resolution process effectively. Ensuring that all stakeholders are aware of and using the correct communication channels is essential for managing the impact of the outage and maintaining operational stability.

Chapter 5: Government and Security Agency Responses

CISA's Initial Alert and Subsequent Updates

The Cybersecurity and Infrastructure Security Agency (CISA) plays a pivotal role in monitoring and responding to cybersecurity incidents, particularly those affecting critical infrastructure. Below is a detailed overview of CISA's response to the CrowdStrike outage:

1. Initial Alert

- **Date and Time:** CISA issued its initial alert on July 19, 2024, at 11:30 a.m. EDT.

- **Content:** The alert confirmed that a widespread IT outage was affecting Microsoft Windows hosts due to a defect in a recent CrowdStrike Falcon content update. It clarified that this incident was not a result of malicious cyber activity but a software issue.

- **Affected Systems:** The alert specified that the issue impacted Windows 10 and later systems, with no reported impact on Mac or Linux hosts.

- **Immediate Actions:** CISA announced that it was working closely with CrowdStrike, federal, state, local, tribal, and territorial partners to assess the impact and provide support for remediation efforts.

2. Subsequent Updates

- **Update on Additional Guidance (7:30 p.m. EDT):** CISA released an updated alert later in the day, providing additional guidance on the impacts to specific environments, including Azure and AWS. This update aimed to assist organizations using these platforms in understanding and mitigating the effects of the outage.

- **Threat Actor Activity:** CISA noted that threat actors were exploiting the outage for phishing and other malicious activities. The agency urged organizations to remain vigilant and ensure robust cybersecurity measures to protect against these threats.

- **Continued Monitoring:** CISA committed to ongoing monitoring of the situation and pledged to provide further updates as more information became available. The agency emphasized the importance of staying informed through official channels and avoiding engagement with unverified sources.

3. Recommendations for Organizations

- **Phishing Awareness:** CISA recommended that organizations remind employees to be cautious about phishing attempts and suspicious communications, which could exploit the ongoing incident.

- **Cybersecurity Measures:** It advised strengthening cybersecurity measures and ensuring that any response to the outage is conducted through legitimate and secure channels.

- **Coordination with Partners:** CISA encouraged collaboration with federal, state, and local partners to coordinate responses and share information about the incident.

4. Future Actions and Guidance

- **Ongoing Support:** CISA assured that it would continue to provide support and updates as the situation developed. The agency remained actively engaged with affected parties to help mitigate the impact and facilitate recovery.

- **Resource Availability:** Organizations were directed to consult CISA's website and other official resources for the latest information and guidance on addressing the outage.

By issuing timely alerts and providing comprehensive updates, CISA played a critical role in managing the response to the CrowdStrike outage, guiding organizations through the incident, and mitigating associated risks.

Statements from International Cyber Security Centers

In response to the global technology outage linked to the CrowdStrike Falcon sensor update, various international cyber security centers have issued statements to provide guidance, assess the impact, and offer support. Below is an overview of the key statements from these centers:

1. National Cyber Security Centre (NCSC-UK)

- **Statement Summary:** The NCSC-UK confirmed that the outage was caused by a faulty CrowdStrike update affecting Windows systems and reassured that it was not the result of a cyber attack. They emphasized that the issue was isolated to Windows environments and did not impact Mac or Linux systems.

- **Guidance Provided:** The NCSC-UK advised organizations to follow the guidance from CrowdStrike for remediation and to ensure that their security measures are robust to prevent exploitation by threat actors. They recommended that organizations remain vigilant and monitor for phishing attempts that might exploit the situation.

- **Additional Resources:** The NCSC-UK provided links to CrowdStrike's technical support and resources, as well as recommendations for incident response and recovery.

2. Australian Cyber Security Centre (ACSC)

- **Statement Summary:** The ACSC acknowledged the global outage and confirmed that it was related to a defective CrowdStrike update. They assured that the issue was not a result of a cyber attack and that they were working with CrowdStrike and other stakeholders to support affected organizations.

- **Guidance Provided:** The ACSC emphasized the importance of following CrowdStrike's instructions for updating and patching systems. They also advised Australian organizations to be alert to potential phishing scams and to verify the authenticity of any communications regarding the outage.

- **Support Offered:** The ACSC offered to provide additional support and guidance through their website and direct communication channels, and encouraged organizations to report any unusual activity or concerns.

3. Canadian Centre for Cyber Security (CCCS)

- **Statement Summary:** The CCCS issued a statement confirming the outage's connection to a problematic CrowdStrike update, with no indication of a cyber attack. They highlighted that the issue was specific to Windows systems and assured that their own systems and operations were unaffected.

- **Guidance Provided:** The CCCS advised Canadian organizations to follow CrowdStrike's remediation steps and to maintain vigilance against potential cyber threats that could exploit the situation. They recommended checking for updates from CrowdStrike and ensuring that security protocols are up-to-date.

- **Resources Available:** The CCCS provide links to CrowdStrike's support resources and additional information on managing cybersecurity during the outage. They also highlighted the importance of ongoing monitoring and incident response.

4. Other Notable Agencies

- **European Union Agency for Cybersecurity (ENISA):** ENISA issued a statement emphasizing the need for European organizations to adhere to CrowdStrike's guidance and to remain cautious of potential phishing attempts.

They offered support through their network of national cybersecurity agencies.

- **Singapore Cyber Security Agency (CSA):** The CSA confirmed that the outage did not affect Singaporean systems and encouraged local organizations to stay updated with CrowdStrike's official channels and enhance their cybersecurity practices to mitigate any associated risks.

These statements reflect a coordinated international response to the outage, highlighting the shared concern for cybersecurity and the importance of following official guidance. The focus has been on reassuring stakeholders, providing clear instructions for remediation, and maintaining vigilance against potential exploitation of the incident.

Chapter 6: Impact on State and Local Governments

Governor Wes Moore's Update on Maryland's Response

Governor Wes Moore of Maryland provided a detailed update regarding the statewide impact of the CrowdStrike-related IT outage. His statement emphasized the severity of the situation, the state's proactive response, and ongoing recovery efforts. Key points from his update include:

1. Overview of the Incident

- **Initial Discovery:** Governor Moore reported that Maryland's state government became aware of the outage around 3 a.m. The issue was linked to a defective update from CrowdStrike affecting Windows servers and workstations across the state. This problem was identified as a software defect rather than a security breach.

- **Immediate Actions:** Upon confirmation, the state government swiftly mobilized resources to address the disruption, with a focus on restoring normal operations as quickly as possible.

2. Progress and Recovery Efforts

- **System Restoration:** As of the latest update, significant progress had been made in restoring affected systems. Most state agencies reported only minimal disruption, with brief outages or blue screen errors that have since been resolved.

- **Automatic and Manual Fixes:** CrowdStrike is deploying an automatic update to address the issue. However, some systems require manual intervention. The Maryland Department of Information Technology is working closely with CrowdStrike to apply these fixes and restore full functionality.

3. Coordination and Support

- **Statewide Coordination:** The Maryland Department of Emergency Management has activated the State Emergency Operations Center and raised the State Activation Level to "Partial." This move ensures coordinated efforts across state, county, and local governments to manage the situation effectively.

- **Collaboration with Key Stakeholders:** Governor Moore praised the cooperation of county and local governments, private and nonprofit sectors, and other key stakeholders. Their collaborative efforts are crucial in managing the statewide impact and ensuring a smooth recovery.

4. Specific Impact Areas

- **Health Sector:** The Maryland Department of Health and associated healthcare partners faced varying degrees of technical issues. Outages affected facilities such as the Division of Vital Records and some local vital records offices. The department is monitoring the situation and coordinating with major medical systems to address ongoing issues.

- **Transportation Sector:** The Maryland Department of Transportation reported disruptions at Baltimore/Washington International Thurgood Marshall Airport, affecting several airlines. Travelers were advised to check flight statuses and expect potential delays. The EZPass system also experienced slower processing times.

5. Ongoing Monitoring and Support

- **Monitoring Efforts:** The Department of Information Technology and the Maryland Security Operations Center continue to monitor the situation closely. They are providing guidance and support to ensure that all affected systems are restored and that services remain operational.

- **Public Communication:** The Governor's office has emphasized the importance of keeping the public informed and ensuring that Marylanders are aware of the ongoing recovery efforts. The state remains committed to transparency and continued support until the issue is fully resolved.

Governor Moore's update underscores the state's commitment to addressing the incident with urgency and efficiency, reflecting the collaborative approach and robust response efforts that characterize Maryland's handling of the outage.

Statewide Coordination and System Restoration Efforts

In the wake of the global technology outage caused by the faulty CrowdStrike Falcon sensor update, state and local governments, particularly in Maryland, have been actively engaged in restoring affected systems and coordinating their response efforts. Here's a detailed look at the statewide coordination and system restoration efforts:

1. Coordination Efforts

- **State Emergency Operations Center (SEOC):** The Maryland Department of Emergency Management (MDEM) has activated the State Emergency Operations Center to manage the statewide response to the outage. This center coordinates between various state agencies, local governments, and private sector partners to ensure a unified approach to the crisis.

- **Agency Collaboration:** The Maryland Department of Information Technology (DoIT) is working closely with state agencies to address technical issues and implement fixes. DoIT is liaising with CrowdStrike and Microsoft to facilitate the deployment of updates and patches necessary for system restoration.

- **Local Government Support:** Coordination extends to local governments and county officials who are working to ensure that municipal systems are restored and that local services are maintained. Communication channels have been established to provide real-time updates and support to local entities.

2. System Restoration Efforts

- **Automatic and Manual Patching:** While CrowdStrike is deploying automatic updates to address the faulty content update, manual intervention is required in some cases. The Maryland Department of Information Technology is facilitating the manual patching process for systems unable to receive the automatic fix.

- **Technical Support Teams:** Dedicated technical support teams are deployed to assist state agencies and other impacted entities in troubleshooting issues, applying patches, and restoring systems. These teams are working to minimize downtime and ensure that critical services are up and running as soon as possible.

- **Monitoring and Assessment:** The Maryland Security Operations Center and other monitoring entities are continuously assessing the impact of the outage, tracking system performance, and identifying any remaining issues. They are also monitoring for any signs of attempted exploitation or further security concerns.

- **Public Communication:** The Maryland Department of Information Technology is providing regular updates to the public and key stakeholders about the status of system restoration efforts. This includes informing residents about potential disruptions and providing guidance on any actions they may need to take.

3. Support for Affected Sectors

- **Healthcare Sector:** The Maryland Department of Health is working with healthcare providers and contractors to address technical issues affecting vital records and medical systems. The department is coordinating with emergency medical services to ensure that healthcare operations continue smoothly.

- **Transportation Sector:** Efforts are underway to address disruptions reported by the Maryland Department of Transportation, including delays at Baltimore/Washington International Thurgood Marshall Airport and toll processing issues. The department is working with airlines and toll agencies to resolve these disruptions and provide updates to travelers.

- **Public Services:** Other state services, including those related to public safety and utilities, are being monitored and supported to ensure that essential functions remain operational. The state is working to mitigate any impacts on public services and to provide timely information to affected residents.

Overall, the statewide coordination and system restoration efforts in Maryland reflect a comprehensive approach to managing the crisis and ensuring that state and local systems are brought back online as quickly and smoothly as possible. The collaboration between state agencies, local governments, and private sector partners is crucial to addressing the impacts of the outage and maintaining continuity of services.

Chapter 7: Sector-Specific Impacts and Mitigation Strategies

Healthcare Sector: Maryland Department of Health

The global technology outage triggered by the faulty CrowdStrike Falcon sensor update has had significant impacts on the healthcare sector in Maryland. The Maryland Department of Health (MDH) is at the forefront of addressing these challenges and implementing mitigation strategies. Here's an overview of the sector-specific impacts and the steps being taken to address them:

1. Impact on Healthcare Systems

- **Vital Records:** The outage has affected the Division of Vital Records and local vital records offices, leading to disruptions in accessing and processing vital documents such as birth and death certificates. This has impacted both administrative functions and public services related to vital records.

- **Medical Systems:** Several major medical systems and healthcare facilities have reported technical issues, including disruptions in electronic health records (EHR) systems, patient management systems, and other critical healthcare applications. These disruptions have affected the ability to access patient data and provide timely medical care.

- **Contractors and Partners:** Health care contractors and partners that rely on digital systems for various services have also experienced operational challenges. This includes issues with data exchange, system integration, and support services.

2. Mitigation Strategies

- **Technical Support and Recovery:** The Maryland Department of Health has mobilized technical support teams to assist healthcare providers and facilities in troubleshooting and resolving technical issues. This includes applying patches, restoring systems, and ensuring that essential healthcare operations are minimally disrupted.

- **Coordination with Health Care Providers:** MDH is working closely with healthcare providers to ensure they receive timely updates and support. The department is coordinating with hospitals, clinics, and other healthcare facilities to prioritize critical systems and facilitate their recovery.

- **Alternative Processes:** In cases where systems are severely impacted, MDH is advising healthcare facilities to implement alternative processes to maintain operations. This may include manual record-keeping, temporary use of backup systems, and alternative methods for accessing and sharing patient information.

- **Communication and Guidance:** The department is providing regular updates to healthcare providers regarding the status of system restoration and any interim measures they should adopt. MDH is also issuing guidance on handling disruptions and maintaining patient care during the outage.

- **Emergency Response Coordination:** MDH is coordinating with emergency medical services and other response teams to ensure that patient care is not compromised. This includes monitoring emergency medical systems and ensuring that they remain operational to support critical care needs.

3. Public Health and Safety

- **Monitoring and Assessment:** MDH is continuously monitoring the impact of the outage on public health and safety. The department is assessing the situation to identify any potential risks or additional needs and coordinating with other agencies to address these issues.

- **Support for Affected Patients:** The department is working to support patients who may be affected by disruptions in healthcare services. This includes ensuring that essential medical care continues and providing guidance to patients on accessing care during the outage.

In summary, the Maryland Department of Health is actively managing the impacts of the CrowdStrike Falcon sensor update outage on the healthcare sector. Through technical support, coordination with healthcare providers, alternative processes, and ongoing communication, MDH is working to mitigate disruptions and ensure the continued delivery of essential healthcare services.

Transportation Sector: Maryland Department of Transportation

The Maryland Department of Transportation (MDOT) has been significantly affected by the CrowdStrike software outage, particularly in the realm of transportation services and infrastructure. Here's a detailed breakdown of the impacts and the ongoing mitigation strategies:

1. Impacts on Transportation Services

- **Airport Operations:** The outage has caused disruptions at Baltimore/Washington International Thurgood Marshall Airport, affecting several airlines. The technical issues led to delays in flight operations and difficulties in processing flight information and passenger check-ins. Airlines have been working to manage the backlog and resume normal operations as quickly as possible.

- **EZPass System:** The statewide EZPass toll collection system has experienced delays in processing transactions. This has led to longer wait times for toll payments and potential disruptions in toll road usage. The impact on toll processing efficiency has raised concerns about traffic congestion and delays.

- **Traffic Management Systems:** Technical issues related to the outage have also affected traffic management systems, including traffic signal controls and real-time traffic monitoring. This has the potential to cause traffic delays and affect the flow of vehicles across major roads and highways.

2. Mitigation Strategies

- **Coordination with Airlines:** MDOT is coordinating with airlines operating out of Baltimore/Washington International Airport to address operational disruptions. This includes facilitating communication between airlines and airport authorities to manage flight schedules, reduce delays, and assist passengers.

- **Alternative Payment Methods:** To address the delays in the EZPass system, MDOT has implemented alternative toll payment methods where possible. This includes allowing manual toll payments and providing temporary solutions to manage toll transactions efficiently while the system is being restored.

- **Traffic Management Adjustments:** In response to the impact on traffic management systems, MDOT is working to implement temporary adjustments to traffic signal timings and monitoring systems. This includes deploying additional traffic management personnel to manage intersections and high-traffic areas to minimize congestion and ensure smooth traffic flow.

- **System Restoration and Testing:** MDOT is collaborating with technical support teams to expedite the restoration of affected transportation systems. This involves testing and validating the functionality of traffic management and toll collection systems once patches and updates are applied to ensure that they are fully operational.

- **Public Communication:** MDOT is actively communicating with the public regarding the status of transportation services and any disruptions caused by the outage. This includes providing updates through various channels such as the MDOT website, social media, and public announcements to keep travelers informed and provide guidance on alternative travel options if needed.

3. Long-Term Considerations

- **System Redundancies:** In the wake of this incident, MDOT is reviewing and enhancing its system redundancy and backup plans. This includes assessing the resilience of transportation infrastructure and implementing measures to prevent future disruptions due to similar technical issues.

- **Collaborative Efforts:** MDOT continues to collaborate with federal and state agencies, including the Department of Emergency Management and cybersecurity experts, to ensure that all systems are restored and to address any ongoing concerns. This collaborative effort aims to strengthen the overall response and recovery strategy for transportation services.

The Maryland Department of Transportation's proactive measures and coordination efforts are essential in mitigating the impacts of the outage on transportation services. By implementing these strategies, MDOT aims to restore normal operations and minimize disruptions to travelers and transportation infrastructure.

Other Public Services and Infrastructure

The global outage caused by the faulty CrowdStrike Falcon sensor update has had a ripple effect across various sectors, including public services and infrastructure beyond healthcare and transportation. Here's an in-depth look at the impact on other public services and infrastructure, along with the strategies implemented to mitigate these effects:

1. Public Safety and Emergency Services

- **Disruption of Communication Systems:** Public safety communication systems, including emergency response and 911 services, experienced intermittent disruptions. To mitigate this, emergency services have employed backup communication channels and are working with technical teams to restore full functionality.

- **Coordination with Emergency Responders:** Coordination with local and state emergency responders has been crucial. Agencies are utilizing alternative communication methods and have established contingency plans to ensure that emergency responses are not compromised.

2. Utilities and Energy Services

- **Impact on Utility Management Systems:** Utility management systems, including those for electricity, water, and gas, have faced challenges due to the outage. These systems experienced delays in monitoring and control operations.

- **Restoration Efforts:** Utility companies have implemented manual monitoring processes and are collaborating with IT support teams to address any issues related to the outage. There has been a focus on ensuring that essential services remain operational and that any service disruptions are promptly addressed.

- **Public Communication:** Utility providers are communicating with customers regarding any potential disruptions and providing updates on service restoration efforts. They are also advising residents on how to conserve energy and manage any temporary inconveniences.

3. Educational Institutions

- **Disruption to Online Learning Platforms:** Many educational institutions experienced disruptions to online learning platforms, affecting remote education and administrative functions.

- **Alternative Learning Solutions:** Schools and universities have implemented alternative methods for delivering instruction, such as in-person classes or temporary shifts to other digital platforms. IT departments are working to restore access to affected systems and ensure that educational services continue with minimal interruption.

4. Financial Services

- **Impact on Transaction Processing:** Financial institutions have reported delays and issues with transaction processing systems. This includes challenges with online banking, payment processing, and financial transactions.

- **Mitigation Strategies:** Banks and financial institutions have employed manual transaction processing and are working with technology vendors to resolve system issues. They are providing regular updates to customers and ensuring that critical financial services are maintained.

5. Public Sector IT Infrastructure

- **Government Agency Systems:** Various government agencies beyond those directly mentioned have faced system outages and disruptions. This includes issues with internal IT infrastructure and public-facing digital services.

- **Restoration and Support:** IT support teams are prioritizing the restoration of critical systems and providing technical assistance to affected government agencies. There is a focus on ensuring that public services and government functions continue to operate effectively.

6. Residential and Community Services

- **Community Centers and Public Libraries:** Community centers and public libraries have faced disruptions in their digital services, including online resources and reservation systems.

- **Service Continuity:** These facilities are providing alternative means for accessing resources and services. They are also working to restore digital systems as quickly as possible to minimize the impact on community activities.

Overall, the response to the impact on public services and infrastructure involves a multi-faceted approach that includes immediate restoration efforts, implementation of backup systems, and clear communication with the public. The goal is to minimize disruptions and ensure that essential services and infrastructure continue to function effectively during and after the outage.

Chapter 8: Workaround and Recovery Procedures

Manual Patching and Recovery Steps for Windows Hosts

In response to the CrowdStrike Falcon sensor update issue, affected Windows hosts require specific manual patching and recovery procedures to resolve the outages and restore normal operations. Below are the detailed steps for manually patching and recovering Windows hosts:

1. **Preparation for Recovery**

   - **Identify Affected Hosts:** Begin by identifying which Windows hosts are impacted. Symptoms may include system crashes, blue screens, or errors related to the Falcon sensor. Use CrowdStrike's query tools or dashboards to locate these hosts.

   - **Ensure Backup and Data Integrity:** Before proceeding with recovery steps, ensure that all critical data is backed up. This is crucial to prevent data loss during the recovery process.

2. Manual Patching Process

- **Reboot the Host:**
  Restart the affected Windows host to allow it to attempt to download the reverted content update. For faster download and installation, connect the host to a wired network rather than relying on Wi-Fi.

- **Access Safe Mode:**
  If the host continues to experience issues after rebooting, boot into Safe Mode or Windows Recovery Environment (WinRE). To do this, restart the host and press the appropriate key (usually F8, F12, or Shift + F8) to enter Safe Mode.

  In Safe Mode, use Safe Mode with Networking to facilitate internet connectivity if needed.

- **Navigate to CrowdStrike Directory:**
  Once in Safe Mode, navigate to the CrowdStrike directory where the sensor files are located. This directory is typically located at `%WINDIR%\System32\drivers\CrowdStrike`.

If using WinRE, navigate to the directory from the OS volume, usually located at `C:\windows\system32\drivers\CrowdStrike`.

- **Delete Problematic Files:**
  Locate the file named `C-00000291*.sys` with a timestamp of 0409 UTC. This file represents the problematic content update.

  Delete this file from the CrowdStrike directory. Ensure that only the problematic file is deleted and no other files or directories are affected.

- **Verify Correct File Version:**
  Ensure that a reverted channel file with a timestamp of 0527 UTC or later is present in the directory. This file represents the correct version of the update.

  If multiple files are present, confirm that at least one file has the correct timestamp to ensure that the active content is the reverted version.

- **Perform a Cold Boot:**
  Shut down the host completely. Wait a few moments, then power it back on. This process

helps in applying the reverted update and stabilizing the system.

3. Verification and Post-Recovery Actions

- **Check System Stability:**
  After rebooting, monitor the system for stability and check if the issues related to the Falcon sensor have been resolved. Ensure that the host operates without crashing or displaying blue screen errors.

- **Update and Patch Management:**
  Confirm that the system is running the correct version of the Falcon sensor and is fully updated with any additional patches or fixes provided by CrowdStrike.

- **Document and Report Issues:**
  Document the recovery steps taken and any residual issues. Report these findings to CrowdStrike support for further assistance and to contribute to ongoing troubleshooting efforts.

4. Continuous Monitoring and Support
- **Ongoing Monitoring:**

Continuously monitor the affected hosts to ensure that the recovery is effective and that no further issues arise.

- **Seek Support if Needed:**
  If problems persist or additional assistance is required, contact CrowdStrike technical support for further guidance and support.

By following these manual patching and recovery steps, organizations can address the immediate impact of the faulty update, restore affected Windows hosts, and resume normal operations.

Specific Guidance for Public Cloud and Virtual Environments

The CrowdStrike Falcon sensor update issue has affected not just traditional on-premises systems but also public cloud and virtual environments. Organizations using cloud and virtualized infrastructures need to follow tailored recovery and workaround procedures to address disruptions effectively. Here's a detailed guide for managing these environments:

1. **Public Cloud Environments**

    - **Cloud Platform Specific Actions:**

    - **Amazon Web Services (AWS):**

        - **Snapshot and Rollback:** Detach the affected operating system disk volume from the impacted virtual machine (VM). Create a snapshot of the volume as a precaution. Attach the volume to a new VM and navigate to the `%WINDIR%\System32\drivers\CrowdStrike` directory to delete the problematic `C-00000291*.sys` file. Reattach the fixed volume to the original VM after the cleanup. Optionally, roll back to a snapshot taken before the faulty update was applied if available.

        - **AWS Documentation:** Refer to AWS-specific recovery documentation for additional details on handling such issues.

    - **Microsoft Azure:**

        - **Snapshot and Restoration:** Similar to AWS, detach the affected disk, create a backup, and mount it to a new VM. Navigate to the directory and remove the faulty file. Reattach the volume to the original VM. Alternatively, roll back to a snapshot taken prior to the update.

- **Azure Documentation:** Consult Azure-specific articles for further instructions and guidance.

2. Virtualized Environments

- **General Virtualization Solutions (e.g., VMware, Hyper-V):**

- **Volume Management:**

  - **Detach and Reattach:** For virtualized environments, detach the virtual disk associated with the impacted VM. Attach this disk to a different, operational VM to address the issue manually. Navigate to `%WINDIR%\System32\drivers\CrowdStrike`, delete the problematic `C-00000291*.sys` file, and reattach the fixed disk to the original VM.

  - **Snapshot Recovery:** If available, revert the VM or disk to a snapshot taken before the faulty update. This method may restore functionality with minimal manual intervention.

- **Virtualization-Specific Tools:** Utilize built-in management tools and recovery features provided by the virtualization platform to streamline the recovery process.

3. Specific Workarounds for Public Cloud and Virtual Environments

- **Automated Recovery Solutions:**

  - **Backup and Restore:** Ensure that automated backup solutions are in place and operational. Use backup data to restore affected systems to a functional state if manual methods are impractical or ineffective.

  - **Cloud Provider Support:** Engage with cloud provider support teams for assistance with recovery procedures and to confirm that all corrective actions comply with best practices for the platform.

4. **Monitoring and Validation:**

- **System Monitoring:** After applying workarounds or recovering from backups, closely monitor affected systems for stability and performance issues. Ensure that all systems are functioning normally and verify that the Falcon sensor and related services are operating correctly.

- **Validation Checks:** Perform validation checks to confirm that the problematic content has been removed and that systems are updated with the correct versions of the content files. Use available diagnostic tools to verify system integrity and proper functionality.

5. **Communication and Documentation:**

- **Internal Communication:** Keep stakeholders and affected users informed about the status of recovery efforts and any temporary measures in place. Provide updates on expected timelines for full restoration.

- **Documentation:** Document the recovery process, including any challenges encountered and solutions implemented. This documentation will be valuable for future reference and for improving response strategies.

By following these specific guidance and procedures, organizations can effectively manage and mitigate the impact of the CrowdStrike Falcon sensor update issue on public cloud and virtual environments.

Chapter 9: Security and Vigilance Measures

Warnings Against Phishing and Malicious Activity

In light of the CrowdStrike outage and the resulting disruption, it is critical to remain vigilant against phishing and other malicious activities that may exploit the situation. Here's an overview of the risks and recommendations to protect against such threats:

1. **Understanding the Threat Landscape**

- **Exploitation of the Outage:** Cybercriminals may leverage the chaos caused by the CrowdStrike update incident to launch phishing attacks, distribute malware, or engage in other forms of cyber deception. The confusion and increased communication regarding the outage can create opportunities for attackers to exploit vulnerable targets.

- **Phishing Tactics:** Phishing attempts may come in the form of emails, messages, or notifications that claim to offer solutions or updates related to the CrowdStrike incident. These communications often contain malicious links or attachments designed to steal credentials, install malware, or compromise systems.

2. Identifying Phishing Attempts

- **Suspicious Emails and Messages:** Be wary of unsolicited emails or messages that request sensitive information, urge urgent action, or contain unexpected attachments or links. These communications may appear to come from legitimate sources but are designed to deceive recipients.

- **Impersonation of Trusted Entities:** Attackers may impersonate trusted organizations or individuals, such as CrowdStrike representatives or government agencies, to gain trust and prompt users to follow malicious instructions. Verify the authenticity of any communication by contacting the organization directly through known and trusted channels.

3. Recommendations for Preventive Measures

- **Verify Source Authenticity:** Always confirm the legitimacy of any communication regarding the incident by contacting the relevant organization or support team through official contact information. Avoid using contact details provided in suspicious emails or messages.

- **Avoid Clicking on Links:** Do not click on links or download attachments from unknown or unexpected sources. Instead, navigate to official websites directly through your browser or contact support for verification.

- **Educate Employees:** Train employees to recognize and report phishing attempts and other suspicious activities. Regular awareness training can help reinforce the importance of cautious behavior and reduce the likelihood of successful phishing attacks.

- **Use Security Tools:** Employ robust email filtering solutions and anti-phishing tools to help detect and block malicious emails before they reach end users. Ensure that all security software is up to date and configured to provide maximum protection.

- **Monitor for Unusual Activity:** Keep an eye on network and system activity for signs of unusual behavior that might indicate a successful phishing attempt or other malicious activity. Implement continuous monitoring to detect and respond to potential threats promptly.

4. Response to Suspected Phishing

- **Report Suspicious Activity:** Immediately report any suspected phishing attempts or security incidents to your organization's IT or security team. Prompt reporting can help mitigate potential damage and initiate a response.

- **Review and Revise Security Protocols:** After addressing an incident, review and update security protocols to address any vulnerabilities that may have been exploited. Conduct a thorough investigation to understand the attack vector and strengthen defenses.

By remaining vigilant and following these recommendations, organizations and individuals can better protect themselves from phishing and malicious activity in the wake of the CrowdStrike incident.

Recommendations for Robust Cybersecurity Practices

In the wake of the CrowdStrike Falcon sensor update issue, it is crucial for organizations to strengthen their cybersecurity practices to safeguard against potential threats and ensure resilience against future incidents. Here are key recommendations for maintaining robust cybersecurity:

1. Regular Updates and Patch Management

- **Timely Updates:** Ensure that all software and systems, including operating systems and security solutions, are updated regularly. Apply patches and updates as soon as they become available to address known vulnerabilities.

- **Automated Patch Management:** Utilize automated patch management tools to streamline the deployment of updates and reduce the risk of human error. Regularly review and update patch policies to keep pace with evolving threats.

2. Comprehensive Threat Detection and Response

79

- **Advanced Threat Detection:** Implement advanced threat detection solutions that leverage artificial intelligence and machine learning to identify and respond to anomalies and potential threats in real-time.

- **Incident Response Plan:** Develop and maintain a robust incident response plan that includes procedures for detecting, analyzing, and responding to security incidents. Regularly test and update the plan to ensure its effectiveness.

3. Employee Training and Awareness

- **Security Awareness Training:** Conduct regular security awareness training for all employees to educate them about common threats such as phishing, social engineering, and other cyberattacks. Ensure employees understand how to recognize and report suspicious activity.

- **Simulated Phishing Exercises:** Run simulated phishing campaigns to test employee awareness and response. Use the results to tailor training and improve overall security posture.

4. Data Protection and Encryption

- **Data Encryption:** Encrypt sensitive data both at rest and in transit to protect it from unauthorized access. Use strong encryption algorithms and manage encryption keys securely.

- **Regular Data Backups:** Perform regular backups of critical data and store backups in a secure, off-site location. Ensure that backup procedures are tested and that backups are readily available for recovery in the event of a data loss incident.

5. Access Controls and Privilege Management

- **Least Privilege Principle:** Implement the principle of least privilege by ensuring that users and systems have only the minimum access necessary to perform their functions. Regularly review and adjust access controls as needed.

- **Multi-Factor Authentication (MFA):** Enforce multi-factor authentication for all critical systems and applications to add an extra layer of security against unauthorized access.

6. Network Security and Segmentation

- **Network Segmentation:** Segment networks to limit the potential impact of a security breach. Use firewalls, intrusion detection systems, and other security measures to protect network boundaries.

- **Regular Network Monitoring:** Continuously monitor network traffic for unusual or suspicious activity. Implement tools that can analyze network traffic patterns and alert on potential threats.

7. Vendor and Third-Party Management

- **Vendor Assessments:** Conduct thorough security assessments of third-party vendors and partners to ensure they meet your organization's security standards. Monitor and manage the security posture of third parties regularly.

- **Third-Party Risk Management:** Implement a robust third-party risk management program that includes risk assessments, contractual obligations, and continuous monitoring.

8. Incident Logging and Reporting

- **Detailed Logging:** Maintain detailed logs of all security-related activities, including access attempts, system changes, and detected threats. Ensure logs are stored securely and are accessible for analysis.

- **Timely Reporting:** Report any security incidents or breaches to relevant authorities and stakeholders promptly. Follow established procedures for reporting and documenting incidents.

9. Regular Security Assessments and Audits

- **Security Audits:** Conduct regular security audits and vulnerability assessments to identify and address potential weaknesses in your security posture. Engage with external experts for impartial assessments.

- **Penetration Testing:** Perform periodic penetration testing to simulate attacks and evaluate the effectiveness of security controls. Use findings to enhance security measures and defenses.

By implementing these recommendations, organizations can enhance their overall cybersecurity posture, reduce vulnerability to attacks, and better respond to potential threats. Robust cybersecurity practices are essential for protecting sensitive data, maintaining operational integrity, and ensuring business continuity.

Chapter 10: Community and Partner Engagement

CrowdStrike's Engagement with Customers and Partners

In response to the recent outage and ongoing recovery efforts, CrowdStrike has prioritized maintaining transparent and supportive communication with its customers and partners. Here's a detailed look at how CrowdStrike is engaging with its stakeholders during this critical period:

1. Direct Communication Channels

- **Customer Support Portal:** CrowdStrike has established and updated its customer support portal to provide real-time information, technical support, and resolution steps. The portal serves as a central hub for customers to access guidance, submit support tickets, and track the status of their issues.

- **Dedicated Support Teams:** Specialized support teams are available to assist affected customers with troubleshooting, system recovery, and any other concerns related to the outage. These teams work closely with customers to address specific issues and provide personalized assistance.

2. Regular Updates and Notifications

- **Blog and Website Updates:** CrowdStrike regularly updates its blog and website with the latest information about the outage, including technical details, progress on resolution, and recommendations for impacted users. This ensures that all stakeholders are informed about the current status and any new developments.

- **Email Alerts:** Affected customers receive email alerts with important updates, instructions, and support resources. These communications help keep customers informed and guide them through the recovery process.

3. Webinars and Briefings

- **Customer Webinars:** CrowdStrike has organized webinars to provide detailed briefings on the incident, address customer questions, and discuss mitigation strategies. These sessions offer an opportunity for direct interaction with

CrowdStrike experts and provide valuable insights into the resolution process.

- **Partner Briefings:** Regular briefings are held with key partners to ensure they are up-to-date on the situation and can provide accurate information and support to their own customers. These briefings also facilitate collaboration on coordinated response efforts.

4. **Collaborative Problem-Solving**

- **Partner Collaboration:** CrowdStrike works closely with technology partners, including Microsoft, to address compatibility issues, implement fixes, and enhance the overall response to the outage. Collaborative efforts with partners help streamline the recovery process and ensure comprehensive solutions.

- **Customer Feedback Integration:** Feedback from customers is actively solicited and incorporated into the response strategy. This feedback helps CrowdStrike understand the impact of the outage from various perspectives and tailor support efforts to meet the needs of different organizations.

5. Transparency and Accountability

- **Public Apologies and Explanations:** CrowdStrike's leadership, including CEO George Kurtz, has publicly apologized for the inconvenience caused by the outage and provided transparent explanations about the cause, impact, and steps being taken to resolve the issue. This transparency helps rebuild trust and demonstrates accountability.

- **Post-Incident Reviews:** After resolving the incident, CrowdStrike plans to conduct a thorough review of the events and response efforts. This review will be shared with customers and partners to provide a comprehensive overview of what transpired, lessons learned, and measures to prevent similar issues in the future.

6. Enhanced Communication Strategies

- **24/7 Support:** During the incident, CrowdStrike expanded its support hours and availability to ensure that customers and partners could access assistance at any time. This commitment to around-the-clock support underscores

CrowdStrike's dedication to resolving issues promptly.

- **Community Forums and Feedback Channels:** CrowdStrike leverages community forums and feedback channels to engage with users, address concerns, and provide additional support. These platforms facilitate open communication and allow stakeholders to share their experiences and suggestions.

CrowdStrike's proactive and transparent approach to engaging with customers and partners demonstrates its commitment to resolving the incident effectively and maintaining strong relationships with its stakeholders. By providing timely updates, personalized support, and collaborative problem-solving, CrowdStrike aims to ensure that all affected parties can navigate the recovery process successfully.

Collaborative Efforts and Continuous Updates

In managing and mitigating the impact of the CrowdStrike Falcon sensor update incident, collaboration with customers and partners has been a crucial element. Here's how CrowdStrike and its network have engaged with various stakeholders to address the situation and ensure ongoing support:

1. Proactive Communication

- **Timely Updates:** CrowdStrike has committed to providing regular updates through its official channels, including the Support Portal and blog. These updates detail the progress of the fix deployment, changes to mitigation strategies, and any new information relevant to affected parties.

- **Transparency:** Throughout the incident, CrowdStrike has maintained transparency about the nature of the issue, its impact, and the steps being taken to resolve it. This openness is vital in building trust and keeping stakeholders informed.

2. Support and Guidance

- **Dedicated Support Channels:** CrowdStrike has established dedicated support channels to assist affected customers. This includes providing access to technical support teams and offering guidance on resolving issues related to the update.

- **Technical Documentation:** Detailed technical documentation and workaround procedures have been made available to help customers implement immediate solutions and understand the nature of the defect. This includes step-by-step instructions for manual recovery and system restoration.

3. **Collaborative Response Efforts**

   - **Partnerships with Cybersecurity Agencies:** CrowdStrike has collaborated with cybersecurity agencies such as CISA and international cyber security centers (e.g., NCSC-UK, ACSC) to coordinate response efforts, share information, and align on best practices for remediation.

   - **Engagement with Technology Partners:** The company has worked closely with technology partners, including Microsoft and public cloud providers, to address the issue and develop effective recovery strategies tailored to specific environments.

4. **Community Support Initiatives**

- **Webinars and Briefings:** CrowdStrike has organized webinars and briefings for affected customers and partners to provide real-time updates, answer questions, and offer expert advice on handling the situation.

- **Knowledge Sharing:** By sharing insights and lessons learned from the incident, CrowdStrike aims to help the community better prepare for and respond to similar issues in the future. This includes publishing detailed analyses and recommendations based on the incident.

5. Feedback and Continuous Improvement

- **Collecting Feedback:** CrowdStrike actively seeks feedback from customers and partners regarding their experiences and the effectiveness of the support provided. This feedback is used to refine response strategies and improve future incident management.

- **Ongoing Improvement:** The company is committed to continuously improving its processes and systems based on the lessons learned from this incident. This includes enhancing update and deployment mechanisms, strengthening communication protocols, and refining support structures.

6. Long-Term Support and Follow-Up

- **Post-Incident Support:** After the immediate resolution of the incident, CrowdStrike continues to offer support and follow-up services to ensure that all systems are fully restored and operating normally.

- **Continuous Monitoring:** The company maintains ongoing monitoring and engagement with affected customers to address any residual issues and ensure long-term stability and security.

By engaging in these collaborative efforts and maintaining continuous updates, CrowdStrike demonstrates its commitment to supporting its customers and partners through the incident. This approach not only helps address the immediate challenges but also contributes to building stronger relationships and enhancing overall resilience in the face of future cybersecurity challenges.

Chapter 11: Lessons Learned and Future Prevention

Insights from the Incident

The recent CrowdStrike Falcon sensor update incident has provided valuable lessons and insights that can help improve future incident management and prevention strategies. Here are the key takeaways from the incident:

1. Importance of Rigorous Testing and Quality Assurance

- **Thorough Testing Protocols:** The defect in the content update highlights the critical need for comprehensive testing protocols before deployment. Ensuring that all updates undergo rigorous testing across diverse environments can help identify potential issues early and reduce the risk of widespread outages.

- **Quality Assurance Measures:** Implementing robust quality assurance measures, including automated testing and validation, can help detect anomalies and prevent defects from reaching production systems.

2. Effective Communication Strategies

- **Clear and Timely Communication:** The incident underscored the importance of clear and timely communication with stakeholders. Providing accurate information about the nature of the issue, its impact, and the steps being taken to address it is crucial for maintaining trust and managing expectations.

- **Use of Multiple Channels:** Utilizing multiple communication channels, including support portals, blogs, and direct customer outreach, ensures that information reaches all affected parties promptly and efficiently.

3. Robust Incident Response Planning

- **Preparedness for Rapid Response:** The incident demonstrated the need for well-defined incident response plans that enable rapid identification, isolation, and resolution of issues. Organizations should have established procedures and resources in place to handle unexpected events and minimize disruption.

- **Coordination with External Partners:**
  Effective incident response often involves
  coordination with external partners, such as
  cybersecurity agencies and technology providers.
  Building strong relationships and communication
  channels with these partners can enhance the
  overall response effort.

4. Emphasis on Security and Vigilance

- **Awareness of Threat Actors:** The incident
  highlighted how adversaries can exploit outages
  and technical issues for malicious activities.
  Organizations need to remain vigilant and be
  prepared to respond to increased phishing and
  other cyber threats during and after such events.

- **Ongoing Security Practices:** Maintaining robust
  cybersecurity practices, including regular
  security assessments and employee training,
  helps protect against emerging threats and
  enhances overall resilience.

5. Focus on Customer Support and Engagement

- **Customer-Centric Support:** Providing
  dedicated support and resources to affected

customers is crucial for effective incident management. Offering clear guidance, timely assistance, and follow-up support helps address immediate concerns and rebuild confidence.

- **Feedback Integration:** Gathering and integrating feedback from customers can provide valuable insights into the effectiveness of support measures and identify areas for improvement.

6. Continuous Improvement and Learning

- **Post-Incident Analysis:** Conducting a thorough post-incident analysis helps identify root causes, evaluate response effectiveness, and uncover lessons learned. This analysis is essential for improving future incident management practices and preventing similar issues.

- **Adaptive Strategies:** Leveraging insights from the incident to adapt and enhance policies, procedures, and technologies can strengthen overall preparedness and response capabilities.

7. Importance of Transparency and Accountability

- **Transparent Reporting:** Transparency about the nature of the issue, the response process, and any mistakes made is essential for maintaining trust and credibility. Clear reporting helps stakeholders understand the situation and the steps taken to address it.

- **Accountability Measures:** Holding teams accountable for their roles in incident management and response ensures that lessons are learned and improvements are implemented effectively.

These insights from the incident provide a foundation for enhancing practices and strategies to better manage future incidents and minimize their impact. By applying these lessons, organizations can improve their preparedness, response capabilities, and overall resilience against cybersecurity challenges.

Steps for Preventing Similar Issues in the Future

In response to the CrowdStrike Falcon sensor update incident, several key steps can be taken to prevent similar issues from occurring in the future. These steps focus on improving the robustness of update mechanisms, enhancing communication protocols, and strengthening overall cybersecurity practices.

1. Enhanced Testing and Validation Procedures

- **Rigorous Testing Protocols:** Implement more comprehensive testing procedures for updates before deployment. This includes extensive validation in a variety of environments to identify potential issues that may not be apparent in initial testing.

- **Beta Testing:** Introduce a beta testing phase where updates are rolled out to a small group of users under real-world conditions. This can help detect unforeseen problems and gather feedback before a full-scale release.

2. Improved Quality Assurance Processes

- **Automated Testing Tools:** Utilize automated testing tools and simulations to check for defects and ensure the integrity of updates. These tools can quickly identify issues that may not be detected through manual testing.

- **Regular Audits:** Conduct regular audits of the update development and deployment processes to ensure adherence to best practices and identify areas for improvement.

3. Strengthened Communication Channels

- **Early Warning Systems:** Develop early warning systems to detect and report issues with updates as soon as they occur. This allows for a quicker response and more effective resolution.

- **Clear Communication Protocols:** Establish clear communication protocols for informing customers and partners about issues and updates. Ensure that all stakeholders are kept informed through official channels.

4. Enhanced Incident Response Planning

- **Incident Response Drills:** Regularly conduct incident response drills to test and refine response plans. These drills should simulate various scenarios, including update-related issues, to ensure readiness and effectiveness.

- **Response Team Training:** Provide ongoing training for incident response teams to stay current with the latest techniques and best practices for managing and mitigating similar incidents.

5. Improved Update Management

- **Staggered Rollouts:** Implement staggered rollouts of updates to minimize the impact of potential issues. This approach allows for monitoring and addressing problems in a controlled manner before a full deployment.

- **Version Control:** Maintain strict version control and documentation of updates. This ensures that any issues can be traced back to specific versions and corrected promptly.

6. Customer and Partner Education

- **Regular Briefings:** Provide regular briefings and educational materials to customers and partners about update processes, potential issues, and best practices for handling incidents.

- **Training Programs:** Offer training programs for customers on how to manage and troubleshoot issues related to updates. This helps build resilience and preparedness in the user community.

7. Collaboration and Feedback Mechanisms

- **Feedback Loops:** Establish feedback mechanisms to gather insights from customers and partners about their experiences with updates and incident management. Use this feedback to drive continuous improvement.

- **Collaborative Efforts:** Foster collaboration with other cybersecurity firms and industry groups to share knowledge and best practices for preventing similar issues.

8. Enhanced Security Measures

- **Code Review and Security Checks:** Implement thorough code review processes and security checks to identify and address vulnerabilities before updates are released.

- **Threat Detection Tools:** Use advanced threat detection tools to monitor for unusual activity related to updates and address potential threats proactively.

By adopting these steps, CrowdStrike and other organizations can strengthen their update management processes, enhance their incident response capabilities, and reduce the likelihood of similar issues in the future. This proactive approach will help ensure greater reliability and security in the deployment of software updates, ultimately benefiting customers and stakeholders alike.

www.ingramcontent.com/pod-product-compliance
Lightning Source LLC
Chambersburg PA
CBHW071941210526
45479CB00002B/770